W9-CRZ-926

WHERE THE BUFFALO ROAM

ADAPTED AND ILLUSTRATED BY

JACQUELINE GEIS

IDEALS CHILDREN'S BOOKS • NASHVILLE, TENNESSEE

*Published by Ideals Publishing Corporation
Nashville, Tennessee 37214*

Printed and bound in Mexico.

Library of Congress Cataloging-in-Publication Data

*Geis, Jacqueline, 1955-
Where the buffalo roam/adapted and illustrated by Jacqueline Geis.
p. cm.
Summary: This expansion of the original verse includes the animals, plants, and
geographical features of the American Southwest. Provides additional information
on the history of the region and the habits of the wildlife.
ISBN 0-8249-8584-2 (lib. bdg.)—ISBN 0-8249-8570-2 (trade)
1. Animals—Juvenile poetry. 2. West (U.S.)—Juvenile poetry.
3. Children's poetry, American. [1. Desert animals—Poetry. 2. Desert plants—
Poetry. 3. Southwest, New—Poetry. 4. American poetry.]
I. Title.
PS3557.E358.W48   1992
811'.54—dc20   92-7733   CIP   AC*

*The display type was set in Contura Open.
The text type was set in Berkeley Book.
Prehistoric petroglyph ornaments were drawn by the author.
Color separations were made by Blackhawk Color Corporation.*

Designed by Joy Chu.

*Petroglyphs are carvings or drawings made on rock by
prehistoric people. Petroglyphs served early man as markers
indicating the location of trails, resources, and water.*

THANKS TO PEGGY AND HERB ZARING FOR
BELIEVING IN MY ART AND PERPETUATING
MY LOVE OF THE SOUTHWEST. AND VERY
SPECIAL THANKS TO ROBIN CROUCH.

– J.G.

Dedicated to the land and to a time when the buffalo did roam, when there were no boundaries, and when life was lived with no reservations. — J.G.

Oh, give me a home
Where the buffalo roam
And the deer and the antelope play,

Where seldom is heard
A discouraging word,
And the skies are not cloudy all day.

Oh, show me a land
Where the tall saguaros stand
And the coyotes and jack rabbits run,

Where the Gila lies still,
As the green rat snake will,
In the warmth of the hot morning sun.

Oh, the cottonwoods grow
Where the dry washes flow
And the young javelinas are seen,

And great ridges of rocks
Hide the bighorn sheep flocks
Till they graze on the mountaintops green.

Oh, give me a place
Where the roadrunners race
And the falcons and hummingbirds fly,

Where the dry, desert air
Warms the prickly pear
In the haze of the afternoon sky.

Oh, show me a land
Where the bright diamond sand
Throws its light from the glittering stream,

As the sun slips away
And it gives up the day
To the shaft of the full moon's first gleam.

How often at night,
When the heavens are bright
With the light of the twinkling stars,

Have I stood here amazed
And asked as I gazed
If their glory exceeds that of ours.

Home, home on the range
Where the deer and the antelope play,
Where seldom is heard a discouraging word,
And the skies are not cloudy all day.

Have I stood here amazed
And asked as I gazed
If their glory exceeds that of ours.

Home, home on the range
Where the deer and the antelope play,
Where seldom is heard a discouraging word,
And the skies are not cloudy all day.

THE AMERICAN SOUTHWEST

The watercolor scenes within this book are painted landscapes of the American Southwest, including parts of Arizona, New Mexico, Oklahoma, and Texas, as well as lower regions of Utah, Colorado, and western Kansas. The United States map above is highlighted to show the exact location of the entire featured area.

GLOSSARY

antelope: The fleet-footed pronghorn antelope is not really an antelope. It is a deer. Native to the plains of North America, the pronghorn is greatly reduced in number and endangered in some areas.

bighorn sheep: Desert-dwelling bighorns are lighter in color than those of the Rocky Mountains. Most of these animals live in protected areas.

buffalo: Actually a bison, the buffalo once ranged throughout mainland North America and is now extirpated, which means it no longer lives in the wild. Today, most of the remaining population lives in isolated, western areas of the U.S. and Canada.

cottonwood: The cottonwood is a poplar tree which lines the streams and rivers of the west.

coyote (ki OH tee): Also called a prairie wolf, the wide-ranging coyote runs in a pack. Coyotes dig for water during prolonged droughts, saving many animals with the resulting shallow water pools.

deer: The mule deer ranges from Canada to the plateaus of Mexico. Feeding on grasses and shrubs, it spends the summers in high elevations and moves down for the winter.

dry wash: In the Southwest, another name for a dry wash is arroyo (uh ROY oh). It is a small streambed or gulch which remains dry most of the time. After a heavy rain, the dry wash fills up and flows very fast.

falcon: The widespread use of harmful pesticides took the peregrine falcon near extinction in the 1960s. They were soon classified as endangered, and today there are almost nine hundred breeding pairs of peregrine falcons across the U.S.A.

Gila (HEE la): The Gila monster is the only American poisonous lizard. This lizard falls into a deep stupor during the heat of the day. It winters in a moist burrow, consuming fat stored in its tail.

green rat snake: This little-known reptile is active during the day, except in the heat of the summer, when it is nocturnal. Ranging from eastern Arizona, south through Mexico, and into Costa Rica, the green rat snake is a rare sight in the U.S.

hummingbird: Costa's hummingbird ranges throughout the southern portions of the United States. In the desert, it feeds on the nectar of blossoming cacti and brushes.

jack rabbit: Ranging from the Pacific coast to the Mississippi River, the jack rabbit favors prairies, cultivated land, and arid scrub land.

javelina (hah vuh LEE nuh): Also called a pecarry (PECK uh ree), the javelina neared extinction, but under protection, it has become numerous again in the Southwest. They run in large groups and grunt and bark as though conversing with one another.

prickly pear: Located throughout the Southwest, this cactus provides food and sometimes nesting areas for many desert birds and animals.

roadrunner: Ranging from southern California, Utah, and Kansas and south to Mexico, the roadrunner lives in dry, open places. Capable of flight, this member of the cuckoo family eats cactus fruits, insects, reptiles, and bird's eggs.

saguaro (suh WAHR oh): A protected plant, the saguaro's blossoms, fruits, and structure provide food and shelter for many desert-dwellers. Its white, waxy flowers open at night and close the following afternoon, and its fruits contain juicy, red pulp and hundreds of seeds.

Author's Note

The origin and author of HOME ON THE RANGE are not known. Edited and adapted repeatedly throughout history, the first-known printing of this poem appeared in a small Kansas newspaper in 1876, under the title *Western Home*.

The closely related *Colorado Home* was printed in 1885, followed by *An Arizona Home* in 1905. Then, in 1908, celebrated song collector John Lomax discovered the lyrics known today, and their music, in San Antonio, Texas.

Lomax brought the song from relative obscurity into national view when including it in his 1910 collection entitled *Cowboy Songs*. By 1933, HOME ON THE RANGE reigned as the most popular song in the nation.

While the official home of these treasured verses is uncertain, they are here adapted to showcase the many faces of the American Southwest, from wide, grassy plains, through harsh-yet-lovely desert, and to the Rocky Mountain foothills.

Concentrating on the desert and its diverse life and landforms, this book features protected, threatened, and endangered species. Bison, pronghorn antelope, and bighorn sheep now live in protected areas, and even the saguaro cactus is not free from danger.

The adaptation of this favorite childhood song simply serves as a backdrop in my own attempt to preserve this magnificent land.

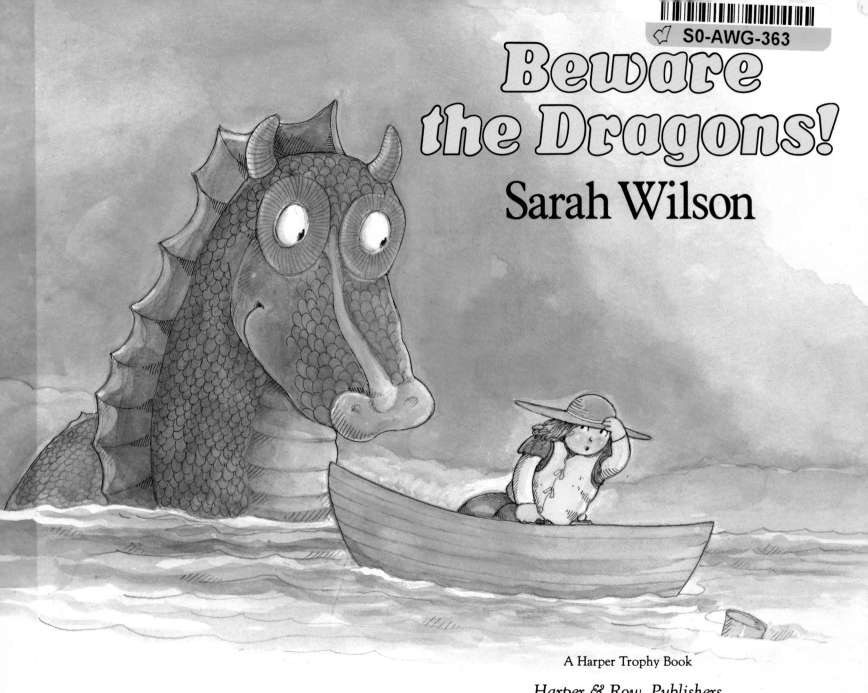

Beware the Dragons!

Sarah Wilson

A Harper Trophy Book

Harper & Row, Publishers

Library of Congress Cataloging in Publication Data
Wilson, Sarah.
    Beware the dragons!

    "A Harper Trophy book"
    Summary: A little girl sets sail across the bay and
discovers that the dragons there, about which her mother
has warned her, only want to play.
    1. Children's stories, American [1. Dragons—
fiction] I. Title.
PZ7.W6986Be 1985   [E]   85-42614
ISBN 0-06-026508-6
ISBN 0-06-026509-4 (lib. bdg.)
ISBN 0-06-443186-X (pbk.)

First Harper Trophy edition, 1988

For my parents

The morning Tildy was to take the boat out alone, there was dragon smoke all over Spooner Bay.

"Great Crying Cuttlefish!" said Tildy. "Why'd they have to come poking around now and spoil my day?"

But by sunup, the smoke had cleared and there wasn't a dragon in sight.

"They're out in the far islands by now," Tildy said. "They won't be back for days! Can I row over to the general store?"

"Will you keep watch for anything green and smoky?" her mother asked.

"Better 'n a keen-eyed gull!" Tildy promised.

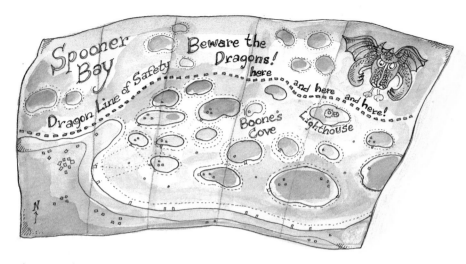

Her mother brought out a map.

"Don't dare drift out near Boone's Cove or toward the lighthouse, Matilda," she said. "Dragons in those parts are as thick as gnats, just set to eat something tasty like a little girl!"

"Haven't heard tell of anybody eaten up yet," Tildy said.

"Doesn't mean there won't be!" warned her mother. "Why else would those fearsome creatures be flying around and around Spooner Bay, scaring folks day and night?"

"Don't know," mumbled Tildy, "but they've hightailed it now, and I've got some sailing to do!"

"Might be some wind coming along too," said her mother. "Maybe even a speck of rain. Row quick, Matilda, and if a storm blows up, stay at the store until it's over."

Tildy was too excited to think about storms. Or dragons, either.

"Right ho!" she shouted, happy to be on her own at last. "I'll be there in the shake of a seal's flipper!"

At first, Tildy rowed quickly.

Then she slowed down to watch some sea gulls.

"Would you like a little lunch, birds?" she asked. "I'm feeling hungry myself!"

With the sun warm on her back, Tildy stopped rowing and forgot all about hurrying, until splat! the first raindrops fell on her nose.

Soon, most of the sky had turned ink dark and a mean wind was gusting up around her.

"Whooeee!" Tildy yelled at the storm. "Where'd *you* come from?"

Things quickly went from bad to worse. The wind and waves carried her little boat on and on, far out into the bay, until suddenly—far from land and smack in the middle of nowhere—the boat hit a bump.

Tildy couldn't see a thing in all the rain and mist.

"Shivering Shark Tails!" she grumbled, keeping still until the storm finally cleared. But when the bump leaned to one side, Tildy sat up, and looked around, and let out one wild whooping yell.

"YEOWWW! DRAGONS!" she hollered. "Great Mustard Greens and Shooting Stars, I'm stuck on a dragon-bump!"

Before Tildy could blink her eyes, the dragons had tossed her out of the boat and up in the air like a sky rocket!

The boat came flying up after her.

"HELPPP!" Tildy yelled, but, except for the dragons, there was no one around to hear her.

Then she heard what sounded like laughing. Dragons laughing. Big hearty roars, followed by lots of bubbling and gurgling.

The laughter grew louder. It was plain to see that the dragons were having a very good time.

Tildy wasn't. Not one bit.

"Leaping Lobsters!" Tildy gasped, shooting up in the air again. And again after that.

When she finally caught her breath, Tildy wasn't scared anymore. She was mad! Red-faced, squinty-eyed mad.

"STOP THAT! You horrible mean nasty bullies!" she shouted down at them. "You wouldn't be so brave if there were folks around to help me! PUT ME DOWN!"

So they did. And with a big splash.

"We're very sorry," said a dragon who introduced himself as Jebediah. "We thought you came out to play with us!"

"PLAY with you?" Tildy sputtered. "Great Snapping Sea Turtles, you're as big as houses!"

"I suppose that's why *nobody* ever comes out to play with us. Nobody likes us!" Jebediah looked like he wanted to cry.

To Tildy's amazement, some of the other dragons did cry.

"It's as lonesome as winter out here with no one to visit!" sobbed a dragon with white whiskers. "Nothing but the wind yowling and no games to play and no new stories to hear, ever."

"So *that's* why you come to Spooner Bay!" Tildy exclaimed. "We thought you wanted to eat us!"

"Dragons don't eat people," said Jebediah. "We eat seaweed and crushed rock and old campfires!" And he started to cry, too.

Tildy felt terrible.

"Suffering Squid!" she said.

"Folks in the Bay don't dislike dragons, they're just afraid. If you'll help me get home, I have an idea how to set things right and proper."

The dragons decided that one idea was better than no ideas at all.

"Please ask the dragons to go orderly, now," Tildy told the old dragon with whiskers. "Too much smoke and fire and roaring around is what gets to scaring folks!"

Bravely, they escorted Tildy back into Spooner Bay. It turned out to be the biggest excitement for as long as anyone could remember.

"Better 'n the Fourth of July!" Tildy shouted to Jebediah, riding up on top like a queen of the sea, waving at the people on shore.

When they reached land, Tildy ran quickly to Mr. Scott's General Store.

"They're really very nice dragons," she said, all in one breath, "not mean and ornery, just lonesome! What they need now is big rubber balls and water kites and rafts. And anything else that floats, please."

Two people fainted.

"Balls and kites and rafts?" stammered Mr. Scott. But he and the other townspeople were too scared to say no, not with a whole bay full of dragons outside. They gave Tildy everything she asked for.

Then, while everybody on shore waited breathlessly to see what would happen next, the dragons began to play—really play—for the first time in all their hundreds of years! They flew kites on their horns. They played slide-the-ball-down-your-scales. They had raft races.

"Well, I'll be a cross-eyed barnacle!" muttered Mr. Scott. "Those dragons look about as fearsome as a pack of pond otters! A mite large, maybe, but what's the harm?"

The other townspeople were shocked and puzzled and then relieved. They began to smile.

Children begged to go out and play with Tildy.

There was a town meeting, later, before sundown.

"Please let the dragons stay," Tildy begged. "They mean no harm. They're just plain lonesome."

Mr. Scott spoke for the townspeople. "About time we had some peace around here!" he said. "For our part, we'll see that no dragon lacks for good company or games."

Everybody cheered.

For the first time in more years than anyone wanted to count, there was nothing to be feared in Spooner Bay.

"Starbursters!" Tildy sighed gratefully. "The day turned out right, after all!"

But the best part came the next morning, when there was dragon

smoke over Spooner Bay and no one seemed to mind.

Least of all Tildy.

She was, of course, a hero.